Po[illegible]n Solution?

Written by Sarah Irvine
Illustrated by Miguel Carvajal

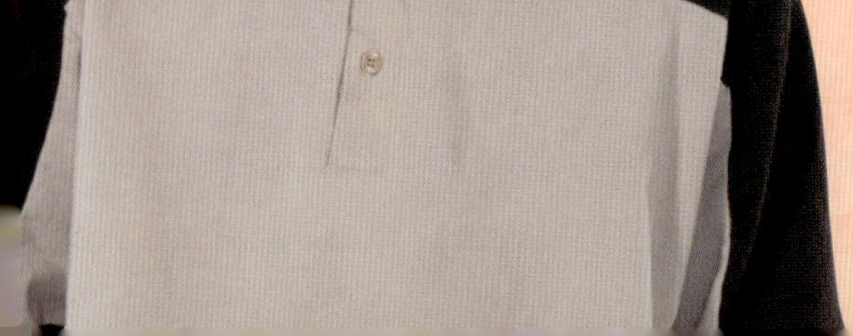

My name is Eduardo. I live in Mexico City, a huge city with 20 million people. Like other big cities in the world, Mexico City has serious problems with pollution. Since the 1990s, the city has been working hard to reduce pollution.

Contents

E-pollution 4

Hola from Eduardo 4

A reply from Africa 6

A reply from China 8

A reply from New Zealand 10

A reply from India 12

What's the issue? 14

Choking cities 16

Spreading pollution 18

Pollution around the world 20

What's your opinion? 22

Think tank 24

Glossary 24

Index 25

Look for the **Thinking Cap**.
When you see this picture, you will find a problem to think about and write about.

E-pollution

Hola from Eduardo

My teacher gave a homework assignment. I need to talk with children in other countries to find out if their countries also have air or water **pollution** problems. If so, I want to hear what people are doing about them. My teacher set up an email network with children from other schools around the world. I wonder what they will have to say.

pollution dirty, unhealthy air, water or land; often as a result of human activities

To: azizi@africa; lei@china; seeta@india; andrew@new-zealand
From: eduardo@mexico

Subject: Greetings from Mexico

Hola,

In Mexico City where I live, air and water pollution are big problems. I am home from school this week because it is not safe to go outside. Wildfires outside the city have made the pollution worse than usual. I am annoyed because I will miss my soccer game this week. I spend a lot of time practising.

Mum had to leave for work early today. She works for the city council and once a month, city officials have to bike to work. Mum usually takes the bus. But because the bus gets stuck in traffic, biking is faster. Sometimes the air is so bad that Mum has to wear a protective mask when biking. Water shortage is also a problem. Many people have only one hour of running water a week. I am interested in your country. Do you have air and water pollution problems too?

Adiós,

Eduardo

In 1989, Mexico City started a 'One Day Without a Car' programme. Residents may not use their cars one day a week, depending on the numbers on their license plates.

A reply from Africa

To: eduardo@mexico
From: azizi@africa

Subject: Re: Greetings from Africa

Jambo, Eduardo

It was exciting to get your email. I was in Mexico City in March 2006. I was one of 107 children at the fourth World Water **Forum**. The World Water Forum is held every three years. People from many countries get together to help raise awareness about water issues all over the world. I gave a speech about water pollution problems in Africa. I explained that about half the people in Africa do not have a way to get clean water. The dirty water makes people sick. In some places, people have to walk long distances to collect water.

Kwaheri,
Azizi

forum public discussion of an issue

To: azizi@africa
From: eduardo@mexico

Subject: Re: Thank you from Mexico

Hola, Azizi

Thank you for your interesting email. I looked up the World Water Forum on the Internet. I found that children at the forum asked the world's governments to make sure everyone is able to get clean water. Water pollution is a serious problem all over the world. More than one billion people live without clean drinking water. We have water problems in Mexico City too. Some people can afford to buy clean water in bottles, but most can't. Mexico City has used so much water from its aquifer that the city is sinking. You would not believe that hundreds of years ago the city was built on a lake!

Adiós,
Eduardo

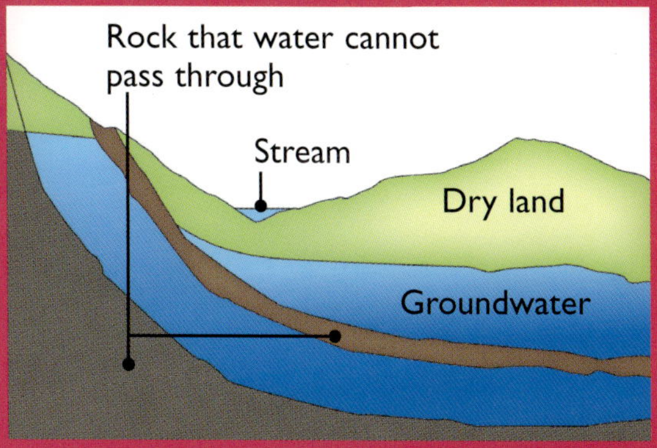

Aquifers are underground beds or layers that contain groundwater. They can be a few square kilometres to thousands of square kilometres in size.

A reply from China

To: eduardo@mexico
From: lei@china

Subject: Re: Greetings from China

Ni hao, Eduardo

I live in Beijing. I have just been to visit my sister in the hospital. She has **pneumonia**. This is the third time she's had this illness. The doctor says it is caused by air pollution. China has bad pollution problems. Experts say that eight of the 10 most polluted cities in the world are in China. The main causes of air pollution in Beijing are called 'the three Cs' – cars, coal and construction. China is trying to reduce the amount of coal it uses. But much of our heating and electricity come from coal. Like other places in the world, we don't have enough clean water. Many factories still pump toxic waste into our rivers.

Zai jian,
Lei

pneumonia serious disease that causes the lungs to become filled with a thick fluid that makes breathing difficult

To: lei@china
From: eduardo@mexico
Subject: Re: Thank you from Mexico

Hola, Lei

Thank you for your email. I hope your sister is feeling better. My mum also has a bad cough at the moment. Pollution can cause many health problems. I read a book about Beijing. It said that in 1999, vehicles in the city had to change from running on petrol to running on natural gas and other types of fuel. This was to help with the pollution caused by vehicles. By 2002, Beijing had the world's largest fleet of natural-gas buses – 1,630 vehicles. I thought that was very impressive!

Adiós,
Eduardo

Natural gas is the cleanest of the fossil fuels. When it burns, it gives off mostly carbon dioxide and water vapour – the same things people give off when they breathe.

A reply from New Zealand

To: eduardo@mexico
From: andrew@new-zealand

Subject: Re: Greetings from New Zealand

Kia ora, Eduardo

Although it has a small population, New Zealand also has air pollution in its biggest cities. Luckily, it is surrounded by ocean, so ocean breezes move polluted air away quickly and regularly. One of New Zealand's biggest problems is a hole in the ozone layer. The layer is in the **atmosphere** about 15–50 kilometres (10–30 miles) above Earth. It reduces the amount of dangerous ultraviolet (UV) light from the sun. Chemicals such as chlorofluorocarbons (CFCs) damage the ozone layer. The hole lets through too much UV light. This can cause skin cancer and damage eyes. It can also damage plants and the environment. During summer, the sun is so strong that your skin can burn in only five minutes!

Bye,
Andrew

atmosphere the layer of gases surrounding Earth

To: andrew@new-zealand
From: eduardo@mexico

Subject: Re: Thank you from Mexico

Hola, Andrew

Thank you for your email. Now I understand that it is even more important than ever to protect yourself from the sun in New Zealand. I found out that CFCs are used in appliances such as dehumidifiers, refrigerators, freezers, air conditioners, heat pumps and water coolers. Now hydrofluorocarbons (HFCs) are used to replace CFCs. But HFCs are greenhouse gases that contribute to **global warming**. I hope that scientists find something better to use instead.

Adiós,

Eduardo

Did you know?

Earth's atmosphere is made up of many gases. Some of these, called greenhouse gases, absorb heat and send their heat to Earth, keeping it warm enough to support life. But some human activities, particularly burning fossil fuels, are increasing the amounts of greenhouse gases in the atmosphere. Scientists are worried that this is causing Earth to heat up too much.

global warming gradual rise in the temperature of Earth's atmosphere

A reply from India

To: eduardo@mexico
From: seeta@india

Subject: Re: Greetings from India

Namaste, Eduardo

I live in Bhopal, India. In December 1984, toxic gases leaked from a chemical plant in the city. It was a terrible disaster. The gases immediately killed about 3,800 people, and thousands more died over the next few days. The plant site has still not been cleaned up. Toxic waste still pollutes the environment and **contaminates** the water. This pollution has caused many more deaths and diseases. My father is very sick. My family and others in our community must travel about three kilometres (two miles) to get clean water.

Goodbye,
Seeta

contaminate to poison or pollute

I received many interesting emails for my assignment. I have learned that air and water pollution are problems in many parts of the world. I hope that we can all work together to solve pollution problems before they get worse and make many more people sick!

Put on your thinking cap

Pollution is a problem in many countries. It takes many different forms. Pollution can harm people, animals and plants.

Think about the questions below. Write down your answers so you can share them with a classmate later.

1. Is there pollution where you live? What type of pollution is it?
2. What problems does this pollution cause?
3. Does pollution affect you and your family?
4. Some people work hard to improve places affected by pollution. What are three things you could do to help solve pollution problems in your area?

What's the issue?

Mexico is a huge country. It has beautiful mountains, deserts and rainforests. It also has big cities. As in other parts of the world, air pollution and water pollution are worse in the big cities. People can get sick because of this. Pollution is often caused by human activities. These include driving motor vehicles, making products and burning fossil fuels for energy. However, modern society needs many of these things for daily life.

The government in Mexico is trying to solve the pollution problem. However, cleaning up pollution costs money. Mexico, like many other countries, is still developing its **industries**. The cost of following the new pollution guidelines may stop businesses from developing. Until recently, there have been few rules about industrial pollution.

industry the making or producing of goods

Did you know?

Fossil fuels include coal, oil and natural gas. People use these fuels in many ways; for example, petrol for cars, electricity in homes and coal for heat. The effect of the Earth warming up from the burning of fossil fuels, which create increased amounts of greenhouse gases, is called the 'greenhouse effect'.

A matter of life and death

Pollution is a growing problem in cities around the world. It causes diseases and kills many people each year.

Air pollution

Chemicals are released into the air. About three million people die around the world each year because of air pollution. Most deaths are in **developing countries**.

Water pollution

Chemicals and waste get into rivers, lakes and groundwater. Polluted water is full of diseases. Scientists believe that more than two million people die each year from diseases caused by polluted water. Most deaths are in developing countries.

Soil pollution

Chemicals from industry pollute the soil and land. These chemicals get into the food chain. They harm people and wildlife.

developing countries countries with little industry and a high rate of poverty

Choking cities

Mexico City is one of the most polluted cities in the world. Exhaust fumes from about four million cars, trucks and buses pollute the air. Like Mexico City, other big cities around the world have pollution problems. The population in many cities has grown quickly over the last few decades. More than 20 cities in the world now have populations of more than ten million people.

These huge cities are often rich because they have lots of workers and industry. Mexico City is one of the richest cities in the world. But this wealth does not reach everyone. Many of the people there are poor.

Put on your thinking cap

Although Mexico City is a wealthy city, about 40 per cent of the people in Mexico City live below the poverty line. This means that they do not have enough money for health care and their basic needs, such as buying food or having proper housing.

1. How do you think pollution problems in Mexico City might affect poor people?
2. What do you think Mexico City can do about the pollution problem?
3. What are some pollution solutions people can try? What problems could people have trying to make these work? Share your ideas with classmates.

Mexico City's geography adds to its pollution problem. The city is in a valley more than 2,000 metres (7,400 feet) above sea level. It is surrounded by mountains on three sides. This traps polluted air. The pollution can make illnesses, such as asthma, worse.

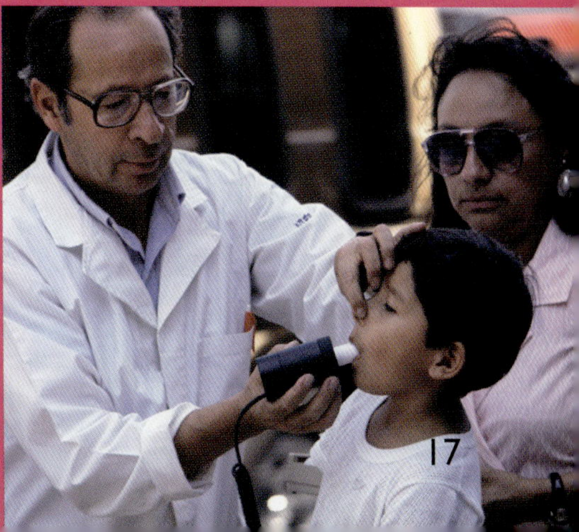

Spreading pollution

Pollution is a global problem. It can do harm far from its source. It travels down rivers, on the wind or in rain. In these ways, pollution can spread from country to country. Sometimes countries have to work together to prevent or clean up pollution.

Many scientists believe that pollution causes global warming. Global warming changes weather patterns. It can melt glaciers and polar ice caps. The average temperature of Earth has gone up about one degree over the last 100 years. Most scientists believe global warming is tied to growing industry. This growth started about 200 years ago with the Industrial Revolution.

These Japanese women marched in support of the Kyoto Protocol (right), and hope for a cleaner atmosphere in the future.

The Kyoto Protocol

In 1997, people from all over the world met in Kyoto, Japan. They agreed to reduce the amount of greenhouse gases that their countries produce. One hundred and seventy-five countries signed the Kyoto Protocol. It went into effect in 2005. However, the United States and Australia did not **ratify** the protocol.

Developing countries often have less industry and fewer cars than wealthier nations. Therefore, they often produce fewer greenhouse gases. According to the Kyoto Protocol, these countries can get 'carbon credits'. They can sell these credits to more developed countries.

1. Why do you think some larger and wealthier countries don't want to sign the protocol?
2. Do you think the protocol's idea will work? Why or why not?
3. If your country approved the protocol, how would it affect everyday life where you live?

ratify to agree to or approve officially

Pollution around the world

Worst nuclear disaster

CHERNOBYL, UKRAINE – About 30 people died when part of a nuclear power station exploded near Chernobyl. However, the **radioactive** pollution from this accident affected as many as five million people. More than 20 years after the accident, people in surrounding areas were still suffering. Many had cancer or babies with birth defects.

Chemicals affect polar bears

ARCTIC – Scientists have found that industrial and household chemicals are affecting the health of polar bears. The Arctic looks clean and pollution-free, but has a problem with pollutants. They are carried on air currents from North America, Europe and Asia. In the Arctic, they freeze into snow and ice. They build up in the food chain and from there into the bodies of animals.

radioactive giving off harmful radiation, such as the energy released from a nuclear explosion

Oil spill mess

GALICIA, SPAIN – When an oil tanker sank near Spain, it polluted about 1,850 kilometres (1,150 miles) of coastline. It was one of Europe's worst wildlife disasters. About 300,000 seabirds were killed. It cost the tourism and fishing industries billions of dollars. The area was cleaned up, but a lot of oil sank with the ship and will continue to pollute the ocean for years.

Dead zones

GULF OF MEXICO, UNITED STATES – Every year, marine life is threatened off the coast of Texas and Louisiana. Spring floods and melting snow wash chemicals and other toxins into the Gulf of Mexico. More than 16,800 square kilometres (6,500 square miles) of ocean have turned into a 'dead zone'. This area is so low in oxygen that it cannot support marine life. There are dead zones in lakes and oceans around the world.

What's your opinion?

People in Mexico and around the world are trying to find solutions to the pollution problem. However, there are some important questions that need answers before pollution can be reduced.

- Who is responsible for pollution?
- In what ways can we reduce pollution?
- What are the benefits of cleaning up pollution? Who should clean it up?
- Does pollution affect only the country that creates it? Should countries be left alone to solve their pollution problems?

People should take responsibility for themselves. Every person causes pollution, so everyone should help clean it up. If everybody did a little bit, it would solve a big part of the problem. For example, people could stop using their cars so much.

I think the only solution is global cooperation. Wealthier countries need to help developing nations. Poor people do not have the money needed to clean up pollution in their areas. All countries must work together.

Think tank

1 Around the world, more and more people are becoming concerned about the pollution in their air and water. What can individuals do to address these problems? What can governments do?

2 How will efforts to reduce pollution affect industries? Will this, in turn, affect the people who buy the industries' products or services? If so, how?

Do your own research at the library, on the Internet, or with a parent or teacher to find out more about pollution issues around the world and how people are working together to solve problems.

Glossary

atmosphere the layer of gases surrounding Earth

contaminate to poison or pollute

developing countries countries with little industry and a high rate of poverty

forum public discussion of an issue

global warming gradual rise in the temperature of Earth's atmosphere

industry the making or producing of goods

pneumonia serious disease that causes the lungs to become filled with a thick fluid that makes breathing difficult

pollution dirty, unhealthy air, water or land; often as a result of human activities

radioactive giving off harmful radiation, such as the energy released from a nuclear explosion

ratify to agree to or approve officially

Inde

atmosph
chemicals
diseases
global warn
greenhouse g
industries
traffic

Index

atmosphere 10–11, 19
chemicals 10, 12, 15, 20–21
diseases 8, 12, 15
global warming 11, 18
greenhouse gases 11, 15, 19
industries 14–15, 17–21
traffic 5